DISCOVER!

ALLERGIES!

I HAVE A BEE ALLERGY

By Kathleen Connors

Enslow PUBLISHING

Please visit our website, www.enslow.com. For a free color catalog of all our high-quality books, call toll free 1-800-398-2504 or fax 1-877-980-4454.

Library of Congress Cataloging-in-Publication Data

Names: Connors, Kathleen, author.
Title: I have a bee allergy / Kathleen Connors.
Description: Buffalo, New York : Enslow Publishing, [2024] | Series: Allergies! | Includes bibliographical references and index. | Audience: Grades K-1
Identifiers: LCCN 2022045115 (print) | LCCN 2022045116 (ebook) | ISBN 9781978533752 (library binding) | ISBN 9781978533745 (paperback) | ISBN 9781978533769 (ebook)
Subjects: LCSH: Food allergy in children–Juvenile literature. | Bees–Health aspects–Juvenile literature.
Classification: LCC RJ386.5 .C6633 2024 (print) | LCC RJ386.5 (ebook) | DDC 618.92/975–dc23/eng/20220928
LC record available at https://lccn.loc.gov/2022045115
LC ebook record available at https://lccn.loc.gov/2022045116

Portions of this work were originally authored by Kristen Rajczak and published as *I'm Allergic to Bees*. All new material this edition authored by Kathleen Connors.

Published in 2024 by
Enslow Publishing
2544 Clinton Street
Buffalo, NY 14224

Copyright © 2024 Enslow Publishing

Designer: Claire Wrazin
Editor: Kristen Nelson

Photo credits: Cover (photo) MERCURY Studio/Shutterstock.com; Cover (art) zotovstock/Shutterstock.com; Cover (art), pp. 3, 4, 10, 14, 20 BTSK/Shutterstock.com; Cover (art), pp. 8, 19, 22 Ava Bitter/Shutterstock.com; Series Art (texture) arigato/Shutterstock.com; p. 5 christinarosepix/Shutterstock.com; p. 7 baismartin/Shutterstock.com; p. 9 Mirko Graul/Shutterstock.com; p. 9 (arrows) Lyudmyla Ishchenko/Shutterstock.com; p. 11 FotoDuets/Shutterstock.com; p. 13 Makistock/Shutterstock.com; p. 15 Andrey_Popov/Shutterstock.com; p. 17 A3pfamily/Shutterstock.com; p. 19 (left) Paul Reeves Photogrphy/Shutterstock.com, (top right) Luc Pouliot/Shutterstock.com, (bottom right) colin robert varndell/Shutterstock.com; p. 21 ESB Professional/Shutterstock.com

All rights reserved. No part of this book may be reproduced in any form without permission in writing from the publisher, except by a reviewer.

Printed in the United States of America

Some of the images in this book illustrate individuals who are models. The depictions do not imply actual situations or events.

CPSIA compliance information: Batch #CS24ENS: For further information contact Enslow Publishing, at 1-800-398-2504.

CONTENTS

I Got Stung! 4

What Is an Allergy? 6

After a Sting 10

Sting Trouble 12

Test and Cure? 16

Stinging Bugs 18

Take Care 20

Words to Know 22

For More Information 23

Index 24

Boldface words appear in Words to Know.

I GOT STUNG!

Ouch! You were playing outside and got stung by a bee! For most people, bee stings hurt when they happen. They will hurt for a little while after. For someone with a bee allergy, though, it can cause a big problem!

If you're allergic to bees, you need to get help right away!

WHAT IS AN ALLERGY?

When the body **reacts** to matter that is normally **harmless**, that's an allergy. The matter is called an allergen (AA-luhr-juhn). The body treats it as an **intruder**. The body makes tiny allergen fighters called antibodies. Antibodies travel around your body in your blood.

Honeybees and bumblebees are two kinds of bees that can sting.

Bees have stingers. The stinger is often pulled off the bee's body when it stings you. It may be left in your skin. The stinger has a **sac** filled with **venom** that gets into your body. The venom is the allergen.

AFTER A STING

If you've been stung, take out the stinger fast! This gives the venom less time to enter your body. Wash the sting with soap and water. Put ice on it. In normal reactions, the area will be red and may itch or ache.

If you are stung, ask a grown-up for help right away.

STING TROUBLE

Someone can have an allergic reaction to a bee sting a few minutes or a few hours after they are stung. A bad reaction might include **hives**, trouble breathing, or **swelling**. Some people feel their throat close up or feel like they might throw up.

Often, bee allergies don't show up until someone has been stung more than once.

A bee sting can cause an even more serious allergic reaction. It's called anaphylaxis (aa-nuh-fuh-LAK-suhs). Anaphylaxis needs to be treated right away by a drug called epinephrine (eh-puh-NEH-fruhn). It's given as a shot—and sometimes people need more than one!

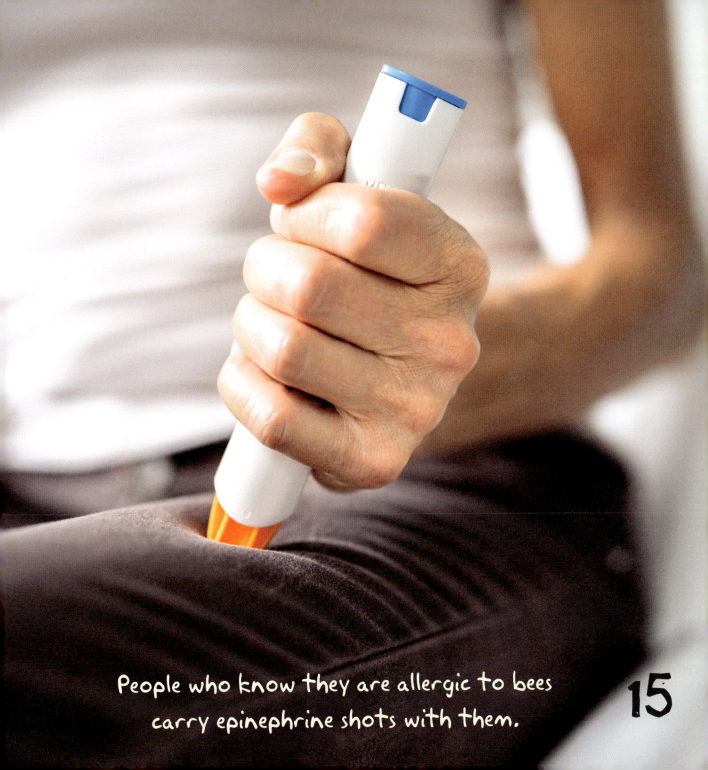

People who know they are allergic to bees carry epinephrine shots with them.

TEST AND CURE?

Unless someone has a bad reaction to a bee sting, they aren't tested for a bee allergy. But, doctors can give a test if needed. Shots of very small amounts of bee venom given every week or month may **cure** the allergy.

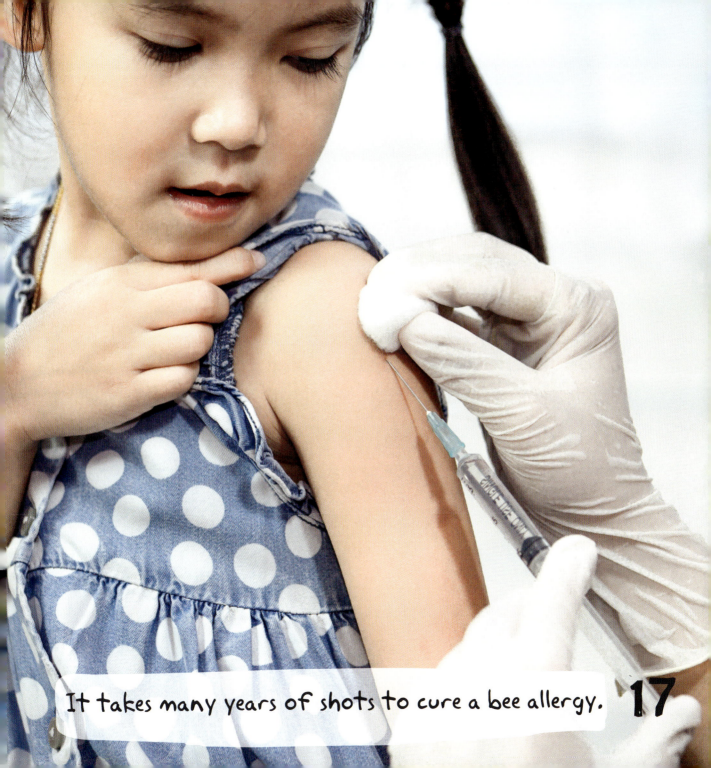
It takes many years of shots to cure a bee allergy.

STINGING BUGS

Yellow jackets, wasps, and hornets are all stinging bugs. They can cause allergic reactions too. People can be allergic to more than one of these bugs. So, it's important to be careful around them all.

yellow jacket

wasp

hornet

TAKE CARE

Having an allergic reaction to a bee sting can be serious. Not getting stung is the best way to stop an allergic reaction from happening! Don't swat at bees that are nearby. Walk away calmly.

Sweet drinks like juice can draw bees. Cover your drink when outside to keep bees away!

WORDS TO KNOW

cure: To make healthy after an illness.

harmless: Unable to cause pain or injury.

hives: Raised, itchy patches of skin that are redder or paler than the skin around them.

intruder: Someone who forces their way into a place they're not wanted.

react: To respond.

sac: A part in the body of an animal that is shaped like a bag and that has liquid or air in it.

swelling: Getting bigger in an uncommon way.

venom: Something an animal makes in its body that can hurt other animals.

FOR MORE INFORMATION

BOOKS

Borgert-Spaniol, Megan. *All About Bee Stings.* Minneapolis, MN: Super Sandcastle, an imprint of Abdo Publishing, 2019.

Duhig, Holly. *Understanding Allergies.* New York, NY: PowerKids Press, 2019.

WEBSITES

Hey! A Bee Stung Me!
kidshealth.org/en/kids/bee.html?ref=search
Learn what to do if you are stung by a bee or other stinging bug!

Learning About Allergies
kidshealth.org/en/kids/allergies.html
Find out more about allergies here.

Publisher's note to educators and parents: Our editors have carefully reviewed these websites to ensure that they are suitable for students. Many websites change frequently, however, and we cannot guarantee that a site's future contents will continue to meet our high standards of quality and educational value. Be advised that students should be closely supervised whenever they access the internet.

Index

allergen, 6, 8
anaphylaxis, 14
antibodies, 6
bad reaction, 12, 14
bumblebees, 7
cure, 16, 17
epinephrine, 14, 15

honeybees, 7
hornets, 18
normal reaction, 10
stinger, 8, 10
venom, 8, 10, 16
wasps, 18
yellow jackets, 18